GOALS AND GOAL SETTING

For Interactive Distribution®

Larrie Rouillard

Distributed by InterNET Services Corporation

CRISP PUBLICATIONS, INC.

Menlo Park, California

Goals and Goal Setting

For Interactive Distribution®

Larrie Rouillard

CREDITS

Consulting Editors: **Linda Sullivan**, **Randy Vetter**

ISC Editor: **Valerie J. Munei**

Crisp Editor: **Debbie Woodbury**

Production Manager: **Judy Petry**

Text and Cover Design: **Amy Shayne**

© 1999 by Crisp Publications, Inc., www.crisp-pub.com
Printed in the United States of America by Bawden Printing Company.

ISBN 1-56052-560-6

99 00 01 02   10 9 8 7 6 5 4 3 2 1

Before we set out on any journey, we ought to know something about where we want to go, how we are going to get there, and when we expect to arrive. With tightly held goals and clearly visualized dreams, success becomes simple.

Success is a progressive realization of a worthwhile dream. You have to work it, you have to go after it. You can succeed if you stay focused on your priorities. Staying focused takes setting goals.

This workbook will help you learn some basic techniques for setting goals to help you stay focused on your dreams. It will show you easy steps for discovering your goals, establishing ownership of them, and using the tactics needed to achieve your goals. I recommend you involve yourself in this workbook. Do all the exercises, write in the margins, look for parts of yourself in it. Then use the techniques whenever you set goals.

Napoleon once said, "I see only the objective. The obstacle must give way!" The great French commander always won the battles in his mind before he even entered the field of combat. With victory visualized, the struggle meant little.

So whether you've been building your business for a long or short time, don't get discouraged if you don't see incredible things happening yet. Success is a process of visualizing your dreams over and over (daily). Refer to your goals. Stick to the success patterns developed in your line of sponsorship. Gradually, as you follow the same guidelines that have led so many before to Diamond and beyond, you can begin to set higher goals, reach greater goals, and accomplish successes you never even thought possible before.

You can do it!

Dexter R. Yager, Sr.

Dexter R. Yager, Sr.

Dedication

To Tina, my purpose and my strength;
to Richard and Carolyn, my guides and role models;
and to Travis and Brian:
may they find an honorable life mission
and make their mark through goal achievement.

—Larrie Rouillard

Contents

PART III: GOAL ACHIEVEMENT

PART IV: SUMMARY

Introduction

Almost nothing is more critical to the success of your Amway business than knowing how to set and achieve goals. Consider this example:

MARY & JACK Mary and Jack Smith were experiencing modest success after two years of practicing the principles of Interactive Distribution®. When they attended their annual leadership conference, they were inspired and challenged by several speakers to set goals—a concept they had never really applied in real estate (their previous profession) or in their Amway business.

They immediately set about clarifying their goals, designing a game plan, identifying potential obstacles and visualizing their success. Each day they reviewed their goals and adjusted their plans. In a short period of time, they experienced a total breakthrough in their business, saw their income double and earned an all-expense-paid trip to Maui!

Before actions are taken, a goal must exist. The goal is a business or personal purpose or the team's common purpose. The goal is the point that you or the team must reach. Only then can you say, "I've done it!" or "We did it!" or "We've reached our goal!"

Setting a goal that really motivates us is not as easy as it sounds; nor should you think of goal setting as too difficult to be worth your while. A single goal's extraordinary power over the direction of your business is what makes setting a goal so important.

This workbook addresses that important process. The activities in this workbook focus on what a goal is and how to set goals you can achieve. Step by step, you will practice how to

- ◆ Differentiate between goals, missions, and objectives or action plans
- ◆ Use a design for establishing goals
- ◆ Construct objectives/action plans
- ◆ Execute the tactics needed
- ◆ Achieve your goals

Your experience tells you that to learn a process you have to practice. You may also realize that learning is easier when you have a purpose. Determining the purposes for goals and goal setting is the first step in your learning these new skills.

WHERE DO YOU STAND?

People who successfully set and achieve their goals will tell you that it cannot be a "sometimes" thing. Consistent goal setting can dramatically impact all areas of your life. In Interactive Distribution®, consistent goal setting can mean the difference between minimum and maximum success.

There is a lot more to goal setting than simply determining, for example, the number of people you wish to sponsor, or even a pin you wish to reach. Goal setting is, instead, a process with several steps. When successfully completed, this process will act as a blueprint for you to clarify exactly what you want and how you are going to get it.

Do you "rarely," "sometimes," or "nearly always" set goals? Begin by completing this self-assessment to see where you stand. You can then determine what you have to do to make the goal setting process work for you!

	Nearly Always	Sometimes	Rarely
1. When I set a goal, I put it in writing.	❑	❑	❑
2. I describe my goal in specific and measurable terms.	❑	❑	❑
3. I visualize my goal on a daily basis.	❑	❑	❑
4. I make my goal achievable.	❑	❑	❑
5. I set realistic deadlines for achieving my goal.	❑	❑	❑
6. I break down a large goal into manageable parts.	❑	❑	❑
7. I look for possible obstacles to reaching my goal.	❑	❑	❑
8. I try to remove or minimize those possible obstacles.	❑	❑	❑
9. I regularly review my progress toward my goal.	❑	❑	❑
10. I identify some personal rewards for reaching my goal.	❑	❑	❑

Purpose of Goal Setting

The most obvious question you can ask at this point is "What's in it for me?" If you can't satisfy that question, that is, if you can't recognize your purpose in this learning process, you are not going to be very motivated to do these activities. This discussion of goals and goal setting is separated into topics to make it easier for you to understand what a goal is and to picture the process needed to set organizational, business, and/or personal goals.

There are actually several reasons to add goal setting to your success strategies. If you ask yourself the following questions, often used by journalists, the benefits of learning this method of setting goals will become clear.

What?	To identify goals
Why?	To learn the importance of goals and goal setting to business success
Who?	To distinguish the people involved in the goal-setting process
Where?	To locate opportunities for useful goals
How?	To effectively reach goals; to accomplish what you want to achieve

The only question missing is *when?* You are the best person to answer that question.

Remember, these objectives are interrelated. They are separated here only for discussion purposes. You have to understand these topics and apply what they require before you can set your goals and achieve them.

Once you understand these purposes, you will see that setting and achieving goals are essential to success in business as well as in life.

Understanding and applying the principles taught in this workbook will provide the foundation for effective goal setting.

WHAT DO YOU THINK?

Look over the following list to see whether you consider the item a goal. Then mark yes or no in the appropriate column.

	Yes	No
Increase sponsoring	❏	❏
Improving productivity in your organization	❏	❏
Managing time more effectively	❏	❏
Seeing the Eiffel Tower in Paris	❏	❏
Capturing the business of an important prospective customer	❏	❏
Reducing operating expenses in a critical area of your business	❏	❏
Reaching a pin level in your business	❏	❏
Developing a new group within an allotted time frame	❏	❏
Learning to play the piano	❏	❏
Planning for your children's college education	❏	❏

WHAT DO ALL THESE THINGS HAVE IN COMMON?

In the space below, write what you think are similarities and differences between the items in the list. (Hint: They are all things that people have shown can be done.)

_____

_____

_____

_____

_____

If you found all of the items on the list are achievable goals, then you might ask yourself questions like these:

"Why can't I...?"

"Why haven't I...?"

"Why don't I...?"

The answer may be that:

♦ You have no real desire to...(manage your time more effectively, become a Diamond, or do what's necessary to sponsor new groups)

♦ If you lack desire to do something, then achieving a GOAL solely for the sake of reaching it will not motivate you enough, nor will you get the same sense of accomplishment

   or

♦ You don't know how to establish motivating, stimulating, functional, and executable goals

So, if you want to improve your performance, get more accomplished, or just see the Eiffel Tower, then you must learn how to set meaningful goals and establish executable objectives/action plans that will help you reach those goals.

On the following pages you will find information and activities which survey the basics of goal identification, formulation, and execution.

Why Set Goals?

Goals are an essential part of successfully conducting business.

Well-defined goals enable choice, design, and implementation of important business activities (objectives/action plans) necessary to achieve overall desired results (missions).

GOALS:

♦ Establish *direction* for ongoing activities

♦ Identify *expected* results

♦ Improve *teamwork* through a common sense of *purpose*

♦ Heighten performance levels by setting *targets* to be achieved

Goals provide the motivation and direction necessary for growth and success in important areas of almost every business. For example:

♦ If you never set goals for direction, how will you know where you're headed?

♦ If no goals exist for progress, how do you know where you stand?

> *and*

♦ If there are no goals for achievement, how will you know when you have arrived?

Question:
Would you get on an airplane if you didn't know where it was going to land?

PART

1

WHAT IS A
GOAL?

Definition of a Goal

Goal—a simple definition:

*"A GOAL is an end toward which you
direct specific EFFORT."*

In this context the "end" is an exact and tangible result you want and are willing to expend effort to achieve.

What kind of and how much effort is always related to the goal itself; that is, you must be able to identify the cost-and-benefit relationship. The way you decide if the goal is worth achieving is through planning and analysis of the elements of the goal. Learning how to examine these elements helps you to calculate the cost-and-benefit relationship.

Elements of a Goal

AN ACCOMPLISHMENT TO BE ACHIEVED

"What do I expect the outcome of my (our) actions to be?" In most cases you will want to express this accomplishment with an action word, a verb.

For example: "I want to increase (our) income from the business to $50,000 per year.

THE OUTCOME (ACCOMPLISHMENT) IS MEASURABLE

"How will I know when I have reached the outcome?" "What are the signs I need to see so I know I have reached the goal?" The situation surrounding the accomplishment has to include things you can use to determine if you have reached the goal—simple, identifiable signs of success.

For example: "In the last 12 months I went from Silver Direct to Sapphire Direct. I'm heading in the right direction."

THE TIME FACTORS

"When precisely do I want to have the goal completed?" Just as important as the other elements are a specific and time by which you will want to be able to say you have accomplished your goal.

For example: "I want to achieve Silver Direct by December 31 of this year."

THE TIME/RESOURCE CONSIDERATION

"What is the maximum time and resources I will allow myself to achieve this goal?" "How much effort will it have taken me when I say 'I've done it'?" The time and resource constraint forces you to place a financial or time value on the outcome.

For example: "This increase in our organization will be achieved by increasing our personal sponsoring rate without lessening our commitment to family time."

The influence of these elements helps to develop the definition of a goal. Below is an expanded definition:

"A GOAL is a specific and measurable accomplishment to be achieved within a specified time and under specific time/resource constraints."

" The importance and benefit of goalsetting is immeasurable. Without setting goals your visions and dreams are just wishful thinking. There are so many benefits in goalsetting. They make decision making easier. Your physical and mental health are better. You have established a positive attitude to life. You are helping to eliminate stress, confusion, and fear. Those who have goals attract respect from people. It gives you a sense of accomplishment. It gives you 'stickablity' and staying power. It is staying power that sets the leaders apart. "

—from **Soaring with Eagles**
by Bill Newman

Goals Must be Written

Putting goals in "black and white," gives more explicit statements of intent and results to reach. Daydreaming about your goals does not help you to reach them. Writing your goals out helps you to make sure you have all the elements for achieving them. It is actually the first of several commitments you will make to yourself to reach your goal.

Look at these written goals.

♦ "Increase sponsoring in our group 15% by December 31 of this year by averaging ten new Independent Business Owners per month"

♦ "Gain 10 new customers and increase personal sales to $1,000 by July 1 of this year by getting referrals from existing customers"

♦ "Sponsor and teach three new IBOs to develop 10 IBOs in depth by June 30 of this year by working in each group two days per week"

♦ "Earn this year's winter incentive trip to the Swiss Alps"

You might think the first and last statements have some fuzzy elements to them. Do they have all the elements they need to be considered goals? What about the other two?

Reread each goal above and turn the page for some exercises.

MARY & JACK One of the reasons Mary and Jack Smith, the Independent Business Owners to whom you were introduced earlier, got off to a slow start in their Amway business is their belief that they could remember their goals without writing them down. Because they were not written, reviewing them to see the progress they were or were not making was inadequate.

As soon as they started writing their goals, they were able to make the goals clearer and were able to post them in a prominent place for daily review.

GOAL ELEMENTS EXERCISE

Identify the elements of goal statements in each of the following:

1. **Increase sponsoring in our group 15% by December 31 of this year by averaging ten new IBOs per month.**

    Action verb: _____

    Measurable outcome: _____

    Specific date: _____

    Time/Resource constraint: _____

2. **Gain 10 new customers and increase personal sales to $1,000 by July 31 of this year by getting referrals from existing customers.**

    Action verb: _____

    Measurable outcome: _____

    Specific date: _____

    Time/Resource constraint: _____

3. **Sponsor and teach 3 new IBOs to develop 10 new businesses in depth by June 30 of this year by working in each group two days per week.**

    Action verb: _____

    Measurable outcome: _____

    Specific date: _____

    Time/Resource constraint: _____

(Turn to page 82 for answers)

GOAL WRITING EXERCISE

With practice, you will learn to easily recognize the elements of a goal. Since you now know what the elements of a goal are, you can learn how to write good goals. Start practicing this skill by writing a simple goal for your Amway business using the elements of goals learned on previous pages.

_____

_____

_____

_____

_____

_____

Now identify the elements used in your goal:

      Action verb: _____

      Measurable outcome: _____

      Specific date: _____

      Constraint: _____

Missions

One of the purposes of this workbook is to help you distinguish between *goals, missions,* and *objectives* or *action plans*. Now that you know the elements of a goal, you will learn how to use some of those elements to shape missions and objectives/action plans. Knowing the differences among these three related types of statements will help you write better statements to achieve your purposes.

Mission—a simple definition:

> *A mission is a general statement through which*
> *a person specifies the overall strategy or intent*
> *that governs the goals and objectives.*

If a goal is a specific and measurable accomplishment you want to achieve, then a mission is an umbrella statement under which you place your goals and related actions.

A mission statement interprets "reason for being"; it enables you to clarify your purpose for yourself and others who are interested. Some examples of mission statements are

For example: "Assist others to achieve their dreams and goals." (a business goal)

"Run in a marathon." (an athletic goal)

"Travel on the European continent." (a personal goal)

Examine the examples above carefully and you will notice that a mission statement:

♦ Clearly states the nature of your cause

♦ Defines your areas of concentration

MISSION STATEMENT EXERCISE

Do you know your mission? Write it here.

_____

_____

_____

Having a mission is an important part of the goal-setting process because a mission helps you focus the direction of the goals. For example, if a sports team's mission is:

"To be the champion of the National Basketball Association"

then a possible goal could be:

"In order to reach the playoffs, beat each team in our division by scoring more points in each half, all without sustaining any serious injuries."

Note: Goals are complementary to the overall mission. But if there were no mission and no sense of direction, it would be difficult to establish any meaningful goals.

A different mission would require different goals. For example, another mission for an NBA team might read:

"It's not whether we win or lose; it's how we play the game."

COMPLEMENTARY GOALS EXERCISE

What are some possible complementary goals for this mission? Write them here.

_____

_____

_____

_____

_____

_____

Now compare your complementary goals and some of the possibilities with the examples on the next page.

Does your list of goals have the needed elements to distinguish each one from a mission statement?

A possible complementary goal:

Mission:	"It's not whether we win or lose; it's how we play the game."
Complementary Goal:	"Play all games scheduled without receiving any "unsportsmanlike" penalties or fouls and without having any players or coaches ejected from a game."

> " An effective goal focuses primarily on results rather than activity. It identifies where you want to be, and, in the process, helps you determine where you are. It gives you important information on how to get there, and it tells you when you have arrived. It unifies your efforts and energy. It gives meaning and purpose to all you do. And it can finally translate itself into daily activities so that you are proactive, you are in charge of your life, you are making happened each day the things that will enable you to fulfill your personal mission statement. "
>
> —from **The 7 Habits of Highly Effective People**
> by Stephen R. Covey

Objectives/Action Plans

You have examined the elements needed for goal statements and learned how mission statements use these elements. The next step is to learn how the elements work in establishing objectives or action plans. Here's how these relationships work:

- ◆ Goals are specific and measurable accomplishments to be achieved

- ◆ Missions are general intents

- ◆ Objectives/action plans are tactics that you will use to reach and achieve goals

The action plans and tactics you use must be complementary to the goal, just as goals must be complementary to mission. For example, if the mission and goal are:

Mission: "Be an NBA champion."

Goals: "Beat each team in our division."

Then complementary objectives might be:

Play Good Defense   "Stop opponent's break away."
"Steal passes."
"Learn about opponent by watching game films."

Execute Offense   "Control the ball."
"Use the clock to our advantage."

Substitute Wisely   "Keep fresh players in the game."
"Stay out of trouble."

These objectives are the steps to be taken to reach the goal. They determine how fast or slow the goal is reached and what methods will be used to achieve the goal.

Goals and Objectives/Action Plans Illustrated

Here is a good visual illustration of the relationship among missions, goals, and objectives/action plans. It can also represent the varied approaches used to achieve goals.

The relationship between action plans and goals depends on which approach best satisfies the specific needs for goal achievement and/or personal preference to reaching goals. There are three possible relationships between goals and objectives.

1. **Several action plans to achieve one goal**

2. **One action plan to achieve one goal**

3. **Several action plans to achieve several goals**

Choosing objectives/tactics that most appropriately fit the desired goals will help you reach the specified goals.

Part I Summary

A goal is an end toward which effort is directed.

The elements of a goal are:

♦ An accomplishment to be achieved

♦ A measurable outcome

♦ A specific date and time to accomplish the goal

♦ A maximum amount of time/resources available to achieve the goal

Therefore,

A goal is a specific and measurable accomplishment to be achieved within a specified time and under specific time/resource constraints.

A written goal provides a strong statement of your intent and the results to be achieved. Goal statements contain these elements:

♦ Action verbs

♦ Measurable outcomes

♦ Specific dates and times

♦ Time and resource constraints

Mission statements define the cause and outline the overall intent or "reason for being" for an individual, an organization or a business.

Objectives/action plans are tactics you use to reach and achieve goals. They must be complementary to the goal and the mission.

> When your plan is well defined, properly pursued goals and dreams direct your life toward positive achievement. No one can set these for you, since they are a personal matter. Each must set his or her own goals and build toward them day by day, week by week, month by month, and year by year.
>
> —from **The Business Handbook: A Guide to Building Your Own Successful Amway Business**
> by Dexter R. Yager, Sr. with Doyle Yager

PART

2

WHO SETS GOALS
AND
HOW ARE THEY SET?

The Process of Analysis

To successfully achieve one's goals requires an internal awareness of the desire and a commitment on the part of the goal setter.

Goal development involves a three-step process of analysis that includes discovery, determination, and decision.

Step 1: *Discovery*–**presentation of wants, needs, and capabilities**

Step 2: *Determination*–**examination of all basic elements**

Step 3: *Decision*–**selection of the goals to be achieved**

The Three-Step Process

Step 1: Discovery

This first step involves looking at your dreams and desires to choose your possible goals. If you're building your business with your spouse or others, all of you need to discuss the dreams and goals you share as you make your list of possible goals.

DISCOVERY EXERCISE

Ask yourself what do I (we) want and need? Make a list of your dreams and desires.

_____

_____

_____

_____

_____

_____

Step 2: Determination

The determination step involves selecting which goal(s) to work on and finding out the who, what, when, why, how, and how much of the desired goal, as well as the expected outcome.

Ask yourself if the goal is achievable—and if not in its entirely, which parts are. Sometimes if a dream or long-term goal is big (like reaching Diamond), breaking it down into smaller, shorter-term goals will make the end goal more achievable.

In this step, data and details of the goal must be examined so that you clearly understand the intent and purpose of your goal as well as what is involved in making it happen.

Step 3: Decision

The decision step sets the ground rules for goal execution and the efforts to be expended for goal achievement. You (and your partners) decide on the costs (money and resources) and benefits (hard and soft) as well as the methods to be used to achieve the goal.

If you're building your business with others, your goals must be shared and agreed upon. Without agreement on a united and concerted effort by everyone involved, the goal may not be reached or reaching it may take much longer than when all parties work together. Success requires that people interact with one another during the goal-setting process. Therefore, the most essential element in the early stages of shared goal setting is *communication*.

Communication

Communication is critical because goals will be difficult to achieve unless everyone involved clearly understands the mission and the goals.

Since everyone doesn't see or hear everything in exactly the same way, deliberate communication increases the chances that everyone involved will understand the goals and direction (mission). Understanding ensures success.

MARY & JACK
Mary and Jack Smith, in the early years of their business, were so busy being Amway IBOs that they communicated little about specifically where they wanted to go with their business. They both wanted the results in their lives that the business could bring, but they each looked to the other to accomplish the tasks required for the business to grow. Mary thought Jack should show the plan much more than he was; Jack thought Mary should sell more products and do a better job keeping the business records in order.

When they finally sat down and set specific goals regarding where they wanted to be and when, they were able to agree on the goals and objectives that each was responsible for accomplishing.

A Four-Task Process

Goals evolve from a discovery process in which you identify an opportunity, dream about a potential innovation, or review the essential aspects of your business or life to find accomplishments that you want to achieve or changes you wish to make.

When you uncover the Who? What? When? How? and How much? of a particular activity, you have the raw material for goal setting.

Goal setting is a sequence of events that enables the creation of attainable, actionable and rewarding goals that lead to positive results.

Creating goals is a four-task process:

Task 1: Identify opportunities for goals

Task 2: Write goal statements

Task 3: Develop goals

Task 4: Formulate action plans

The pages that follow describe each of these goal-setting tasks.

Task 1: Identify Opportunities for Goals

Questions: Where are specific goals found?

                  Where do you find the best opportunities for creating goals?

Answer: All around you!

Opportunities can be found in your personal life or in your business life. Goals can be anything associated with your business or personal life so long as they contribute to an organizational or individual mission (reason for being).

Find goals for yourself. Consider both internal and external factors as opportunities for goal creation.

PERSONAL DESIRES

Goals develop from "seeds": ideas, wants, needs, and desires. Each seed can produce many individuals goals.

For example: "I would like to learn a foreign language so that I can travel to different parts of the world to experience new cultures and develop an international business."

This one desire contains the seeds for many possible goals:

- ♦ Learn a foreign language

- ♦ Travel to other parts of the world

- ♦ Experience new cultures

- ♦ Develop an international business

These desires can be transformed into a goal statement that leads to achievement of the goal itself.

For example: "I will enroll in a six-month foreign language course in the next 3 months and become proficient enough in the language to carry on a conversation within one year."

                  or

"I will make reservations to travel to _____ by the end of March next year at a cost not to exceed $_____."

PERSONAL DESIRES EXERCISE

Each of these goal statements provides the material necessary for shaping additional action plans and formulating tasks to achieve the goal.

Write a personal desire here.

_____

_____

_____

_____

_____

_____

_____

_____

_____

What are some of the potential "seeds" for goals that you can develop from this personal desire?

1. _____

_____

2. _____

_____

3. _____

_____

4. _____

_____

BUSINESS DESIRES

Like personal desires, business desires provide "seeds" for growth.

For example: "I would like to build a large enough organization to achieve a higher pin level and increase my bonuses."

Again, this one statement has numerous potential goals that could be acted upon:

- ♦ Increase sponsoring
- ♦ Achieve a higher pin level
- ♦ Increase bonuses

Each idea can become a distinct goal statement.

For example: "Show the business plan a minimum of 25 times each month for the next year."

or

"Help each IBO in my organization to increase business volume by 20% each month through showing the business plan and setting up customers."

BUSINESS DESIRE EXERCISE

Write a business desire here.

_____

_____

_____

_____

_____

_____

_____

_____

What are some of the potential goals you can develop from this business desire?

1. _____
   _____

2. _____
   _____

3. _____
   _____

4. _____
   _____

Goals are meant to establish direction for you and your business. They provide a firm foundation for building a set of tactics (objectives/action plans) necessary to accomplish the goal.

> " To begin with the end in mind means to start with a clear understanding of your destination. It means to know where you're going so that you better understand where you are now and so that the steps you take are always in the right direction. "
>
> —from **The 7 Habits of Highly Successful People**
> by Stephen R. Covey

GOAL IDENTIFICATION VS. GOAL DEVELOPMENT

In the goal identification phase, it's not important to establish all the details involved with goal achievement or to determine the exact objectives needed to succeed. Those elements are part of goal development (discussed later).

The object of this phase is to identify where you want you and/or your business to be in one, two, or five years. The primary objective of goal identification is to give substance your dreams and desires.

Goals are destinations that not only survey where your business or you personally have been and are now, but they also combine relevant knowledge with dreams and desires to set a direction for the future.

Focus your attention on the ultimate destination. Objectives/action plans, or milestones are only steps toward the goal. The specific action plans may change as progress toward the goal is made, but the goal itself, once it is established, should remain unchanged.

For example: "If the mission is to 'experience many different cultures' and the goal is 'to travel around the world,' then the various destinations (objectives) may change because of travel constraints, the desire to see places not on the original itinerary or expense, but the original goal—to travel around the world—will not change."

GOAL IDENTIFICATION EXERCISE

On the lines below, write down one personal goal that you want to achieve in the next 12 months.

_____

_____

Now list three action plans that you will use to identify that you are making progress toward your goal.

1. _____

   _____

2. _____

   _____

3. _____

   _____

GOAL TYPES

When you are identifying goals, it is helpful to categorize different goals by type. This clarifies their importance to the mission. There are three types of goals, each of which differ in the contribution they make to the declared mission:

1. **Essential goals are necessary for continued, ongoing progress.**

2. **Problem-solving goals propose a more appropriate or desired condition.**

3. **Innovative goals make something good even better.**

When you understand goal types, you will be able to identify the possible opportunities that are all around and you will be able to determine the relative importance of the opportunity to you or your business.

Let's investigate goal types in more detail.

1. Essential Goals

An essential goal identifies everyday activities that require improvement and must be fulfilled to ensure successful results. Essential goals are the recurring, ongoing, repetitious, and necessary activities of business or personal life. These activities are essential to ongoing success.

For example: "Check the supply of literature to use in contacting potential IBOs and order needed brochures."

ESSENTIAL GOALS EXERCISE

Can you think of an essential goal that you must accomplish on a regular basis? (Hint: "Getting up on time tomorrow" may be part of an essential goal, if it's to ensure you'll be on time for an important meeting.) Write it here.

Sources of essential goals can usually be found in one's area of responsibility. Assess the tasks you're responsible for to uncover those elements that must be dealt with on a regular basis.

For example: If your responsibility is talking to ten potential prospects per week, then you must set goals for specific activities such as: create and maintain a prospect list, timing considerations and effective telephone scripts.

Essential goals are those that must get accomplished on a routine basis.

2. Problem-Solving Goals

A problem-solving goal identifies a current problem or opportunity along with a more appropriate or desired condition. It is a statement of a current and future situation once a solution is implemented.

Problem-solving goals outline the activities necessary to improve performance. They are vital to growth, but may not be detrimental if not accomplished.

For example: "Reduce the number of "no shows" in the in-home business plan meetings class from 50% to 20% by the end of this year by training IBOs on contacting and inviting at the next two seminars."

This statement outlines the problem (50% "no shows" in business plan meetings), and the more appropriate or desired condition (only 20% "no shows") that needs to be achieved.

PROBLEM-SOLVING GOAL EXERCISE

Can you think of a problem-solving goal that ought to be accomplished? Write it here.

_____

_____

_____

_____

Sources for problem-solving goals are:

♦ Aspects of the task that can be improved, such as appointment setting, business posture, efficiency

♦ Less-than-effective use of time or resources

♦ Fear of the telephone that can be eliminated or minimized

Ask yourself: What's involved in solving these problems? The answer to this question can provide the seeds for developing problem-solving goals.

3. Innovative Goals

An innovative goal improves the current condition. Innovative goals are not problems, but rather the result of thinking about making something good even better. They identify activities to be done better, faster, cheaper, easier, or more safely.

For example: "Increase customer referrals by developing a system that will get me two referrals from each person in my customer base this year."

This statement says that there may be nothing at all wrong with the current condition, but that if improvements could be made, then the system would be better and new customers could be identified easily than before.

INNOVATIVE GOAL EXERCISE

Create an innovative goal that would be nice to do and write it here.

_____

_____

Innovative goals are sometimes the more pleasurable type of goals to create because they represent our dreams more than our needs.

Other Potential Areas

Many other aspects for business or personal life can provide opportunities for goal creation, such as:

♦ Self-improvement. Self-improvement may mean finding additional areas of interest or new responsibilities to be added over your lifetime. These are personal goals that you may want to accomplish in one year, two years, or five years from now. Setting intermediary essential or innovative goals can help you attain these personal goals.

♦ Market conditions. Analyze the needs of your market area to create problem-solving or innovative goals. Analyze customer needs, uncover market weaknesses, and identify product advantages. Develop goals from the limits of each type.

RECAP OF TASK 1

♦ Goals can be anything so long as they contribute to your mission (reason for being)

♦ Goals identify the direction of your organization or you personally; they are the ultimate "destinations" of our dreams, needs, and desires

♦ Goals are developed from ideas, wants, needs, and desires. They can come from our business or our personal lives

♦ Goals should not change once they are set. However, objectives to reaching goals can and should change as conditions change

♦ Essential goals must be accomplished for your success

♦ Problem-solving goals ought to be done to correct ineffective conditions and thereby produce better results

♦ Innovative goals are those we would like to do in order to make something good even better (faster, cheaper, safer, or easier)

Essential goals should not be passed over the achieve the relatively less important problem-solving or innovative goals. Innovative or problem-solving goals should not jeopardize your ability to achieve essential goals.

Try to find opportunities to achieve multiple goals by completing action plans that are common to two or more goals. Obviously, this requires careful planning and written statements that you can mix and match as needed.

" When you create a set of goals to achieve your dream, you're setting yourself up for success. Maybe you'll hit the bull's-eye. But even if you don't, you'll likely score higher than if you'd never aimed for the target at all. "

—from **Everything I Know at the Top
I Learned at the Bottom**
by Dexter R. Yager Sr. and Ron Ball

Remember: The purpose of the identification task is solely to uncover the wants, needs, and desires for future personal or business accomplishments.

Personal desire: "I would like to learn a foreign language so that I can travel to different parts of the world to experience new cultures and develop an international business."

Goal 'seeds': "Learn the French language."
"Travel to France and experience French culture."
"See the Eiffel Tower."
"Sponsor an Emerald group in France."

Goal type: Innovative—Nice to do. "It would be nice to know how to speak French while traveling in France. My business development and travel would be much easier if I knew the language."

Goal objective: Self-improvement.

" A goal is an objective, a purpose. A goal is more than a dream; it's a dream being acted upon. A goal is more than a hazy 'Oh, I wish I could.' A goal is a clear 'This is what I'm working toward'. "

—from **The Magic of Thinking Big**
by David J. Schwartz

Task 2: Writing Goal Statements

A well-defined goal statement is the foundation for goal achievement. The goal is only as good as its statement of desire and intent to:

- Fulfill one's responsibilities
- Solve a problem
- Be creative and innovative
- Develop a bigger business
- Improve my personal life

A goal statement formalizes:

- What is to be accomplished
- Who will be involved
- When the activity will be completed
- How much time and resources will be invested

The "S.M.A.R.T." way to ensure all these elements of a well-defined goal are included in each goal statement. The S.M.A.R.T. goal statement is:

S pecific

M easurable

A ction-oriented

R ealistic

T ime and resource-constrained

A goal statement that contains each of these elements will provide an excellent basis for setting and monitoring progress and achieving the goal.

S.M.A.R.T. GOALS ARE SPECIFIC

Specific means detailed, particular, or focused. A goal is specific when everyone knows exactly what is to be achieved and accomplished. Being specific means spelling out the details of the goal.

For example: "Increase sponsoring" is too general for a goal statement because it does not provide any specific information about what is to be accomplished.

"Increase personal sponsorship…" is more specific because it narrows the scope of the desired outcome.

Specifying the expected end result is the first step toward creating a S.M.A.R.T. goal.

MARY & JACK Once Mary and Jack Smith realized that writing down specific goals for their business was necessary, they began to see results. They began to understand that helping people in their organization meant helping them realize the importance of setting specific goals. By setting specific goals that could be measured, IBOs were motivated to set other goals that would cause more "stretch" to reach the goals.

Mary and Jack began to coach others to evaluate their goals according to the S.M.A.R.T. goals standard. They encouraged new IBOs to begin early to check each goal to see if it was specific, measurable, action-oriented, realistic, and time- and resource-constrained. Seeing results caused everyone in the business to believe they could reach the goals they set.

SPECIFIC GOALS EXERCISE

Rate the following statements. Are they specific enough to spell out the details of the desired goal? After you complete this exercise, check your answers on page 82.

		Too General	Not Specific Enough	More Specific
A.	Wash and clean the car.	❏	❏	❏
B.	Wash and clean the car each week.	❏	❏	❏
C.	Wash and clean the car inside and out each week.	❏	❏	❏
D.	Show the business plan more.	❏	❏	❏
E.	Show the business plan several times each week.	❏	❏	❏
F.	Show the business plan at least 5 times each week.	❏	❏	❏
G.	Read books and listen to tapes more often.	❏	❏	❏
H.	Read books and listen to types every day.	❏	❏	❏
I.	Read a positive book at least 30 minutes each day and listen to at least one tape about the business each day.	❏	❏	❏

Write an example of a specific end result.

_____

_____

_____

_____

_____

_____

S.M.A.R.T. GOALS ARE MEASURABLE

Measurable goals are quantifiable. A measurable goal provides a standard for comparison, the means to an end, a specific result; it is limiting. Each goal must be measurable—it must have a method for comparison that indicates when the goal is reached. Doing something "better," or "more accurately," or even "precisely" does not provide the quantifiable measurement necessary to determine goal achievement. These words are too ambiguous for a measurable outcome.

For example: "Increase my personal sponsoring…" is a specific statement, but to be measurable, it needs the addition of "… to 15 new IBOs per year."

The words "15 new IBOs per year" provide a standard for comparison and progress measurement.

Tracking the sponsor activity each month will indicate when and where progress is made toward the goal and will determine when the 15 new IBOs per year goal is reached; this provides a measurable limit for the goal.

MEASURABLE GOALS EXERCISE

Check Yes or No to indicate whether each of the following is a measurable outcome. After you complete this exercise, check your answers on page 83.

	Yes	No
A. Provide better service to all my customers.	❏	❏
B. Answer every call received within two work days.	❏	❏
C. Significantly reduce the number of order errors.	❏	❏
D. Lower the number of order errors by 50% of current levels.	❏	❏
E. Add only very productive IBOs to my personal group.	❏	❏

Remember: Measurable statements must be quantifiable, a standard for comparison and limiting.

Write a measurable statement here:

S.M.A.R.T. GOALS ARE ACTION-ORIENTED

Action-oriented means that the goal statements indicate an activity, a performance, an operation, or something that produces results. Action-oriented goal statements tell what is to be done to reach the goal. This action is indicated by use of an action verb. Action verbs describe the type of activity to be performed. Here are some examples of action verbs:

- ◆ evaluate
- ◆ appraise
- ◆ inform

- ◆ investigate
- ◆ influence
- ◆ restrict

In the statement: "Increase my personal sponsoring," the verb *increase* indicates that the expected result is to raise the amount from the existing level to a more desirable level.

ACTION-ORIENTED GOALS EXERCISE

What are some other action-oriented verbs that indicate expected performance?

_____

_____

_____

> "Most of all, winners know that the most important time frames are the groups of minutes in every day. Most people waste most of their waking hours going through the motions, chatting idly, shuffling papers, putting off decisions, reacting, majoring in minors, and concentrating on trivia. They spend their time on low-priority, tension-relieving projects, rather than high-priority, goal-achieving activities. Since they have failed to plan, they are planning to fail by default."
>
> —from **The Winner's Edge**
> by Denis Waitley

S.M.A.R.T GOALS ARE REALISTIC

Realistic goals are practical, achievable, and possible. Goals must motivate people to improve and to reach for attainable ends. For a goal to be motivational, the goal-seeker must feel that the goal can be achieved ("I can do it!"). This realization must occur before effort and energy are applied toward reaching the goal.

For example: "Increasing my personal sponsoring to 15 new IBOs per year" is possible and achievable (realistic) only if the current level of output is 1–2 new IBOs per month. If the current level is only 1 new IBO per month, the "15 new IBOs per year" may not be realistic.

Impossible goals demotivate and defeat the goal-setting process. No one strives for goals that cannot be reached. Goals should not be too easy, either. Easy goals do not motivate any more than unattainable goals.

Realistic goals are a balance between what is hard and what is easy to achieve. They require a "stretch" that reaches beyond what is easily achieved and establishes a more challenging goal. It's that little bit extra in performance that makes people progress and improve. "Stretching" creates the necessary balance between the effort required to achieve the goal and the probability of success.

Challenging, realistic goals motivate and encourage higher levels of performance.

> " Every truly worthwhile achievement of excellence has a price tag. The question you must answer for yourself is, 'How much am I willing to pay in hard work, patience, sacrifice, and endurance to be a person of excellence?' Your answer is important, because the cost is great. But if you are willing to be the person you were meant to be, I think you will discover that for you the sky is the limit. "

—from **The Pursuit of Excellence**
by Ted W. Engstrom

REALISTIC GOALS EXERCISE

Realistic goals are practical, achievable and possible. Are the following goal components realistic?

	Realistic	Unrealistic
A. Swim a mile.	❏	❏
B. Swim across the Pacific Ocean.	❏	❏
C. Hold your breath until you faint.	❏	❏
D. Learn to play the piano in one year.	❏	❏

(Check your answers with those of the author's on page 83)

THE STRETCH PRINCIPLE EXERCISE

How does the "stretch" principle apply to a new IBO who would like to reach Direct?

_____

_____

_____

_____

_____

_____

_____

_____

(Check your answers with those of the author's on page 84)

S.M.A.R.T. GOALS ARE TIME- AND RESOURCE-CONSTRAINED

Time- and resource-constrained means scheduled, regulated by time and resources to be expended, a finite duration to the action allowed, a deadline. People generally put off doing things if no deadline is set because human nature always finds something else to do that has a higher priority.

Time constraints encourage action to get activities completed. Deadlines encourage activity.

For example: "Increase my personal sponsoring to 15 new IBOs per year by March of this year, without working the business on Sundays."

The precise date provides a deadline, while the "without working the business on Sundays" places a limit on the time resources to use to achieve the goal.

Time constraints and deadlines must be precise to promote the urgency needed to move toward goal achievement.

For example: "By the end of October" is more specific than "toward the end of October." But it is not as precise as, "by 10:00 a.m. on October 31, in a specific year." This deadline leaves no doubt about when the goal should be achieved.

The goal statement must contain resource constraints in order to ensure that there is a practical cost/benefit to goal achievement.

> " Divide each dream into smaller, achievable immediate goals. Let's take a hypothetical situation. Say your dream is to lose ten pounds. Start by writing that down on a piece of paper. Next, divide that dream into smaller goals. Perhaps that means losing two pounds a week for the next five weeks. So you really have five smaller goals—two pounds each week for five weeks. "
>
> —from **Everything I Know at the Top I Learned at the Bottom**
> by Dexter R. Yager Sr. and Ron Ball

TIME-CONSTRAINED GOALS EXERCISE

Which of the following phrases represent deadlines and which are just expressions of time?

Deadline?	Yes	No
A. Next week	❏	❏
B. Next Thursday by noon	❏	❏
C. As soon as possible	❏	❏
D. First thing Monday morning	❏	❏
E. Before the close of business today	❏	❏
F. Before the close of business today, at 5:00 p.m. PST	❏	❏
G. December 31, 1999	❏	❏

Write three of your own precise deadlines below.

_____

_____

_____

_____

_____

_____

(Check your answers with those of the author's on page 84.)

RECAP OF TASK 2

S.M.A.R.T. goals ensure that all the necessary elements are included for creating actionable, well-planned, and achievable goals. The S.M.A.R.T. goal is:

Specific

- ◆ Detailed, particular, focused
- ◆ "Increase my personal sponsoring…"

Measurable

- ◆ Quantifiable, a standard for comparison, the means to a specific result, limiting
- ◆ "…to 15 new IBOs per year."

Action-oriented

- ◆ Performing, operating, producing results
- ◆ "Increase… completed…"

Realistic

- ◆ Practical, achievable, accurate, possible
- ◆ "(Increase)…from current level (1 per month) to 15 new IBOs per year."

Time- and Resource-constrained

- ◆ Schedule, regulated by time, a finite duration of activity, extent of resources allowed, deadline
- ◆ "By March 31, this year, without working the business on Sundays."

Task 3: Develop Goals

Identifying opportunities (Task 1) and creating S.M.A.R.T. goal statements (Task 2) are two essential elements needed to complete Task 3, goal development.

Goal development expands goal statements to provide context and substance for expected results and benefits. It identifies the importance, effort, benefits, and results of each statement created.

Completion of Task 1 (Identify…) and Task 2 (Goal statements) may result in one, two, ten, or fifty legitimate goal statements that will require development (Task 3) before the necessary activities toward goal achievement can begin.

You should complete goal development for every legitimate goal statement created. There are five steps to effective goal development:

1. **Classify goals by type.**

2. **Prioritize within each type.**

3. **Establish standards of performance.**

4. **Identify obstacles to goal achievement.**

5. **Determine "W.I.I.F.M." (What's In It For Me?).**

Each of these important and necessary steps to goal development is described in the following pages.

CLASSIFY GOALS BY TYPE

The classification of goals requires a review of each goal statement to determine whether the end result (accomplishment to be achieved) is:

- ◆ Essential—it is required for the operation of the business or for personal improvement. It must be done.

- ◆ Problem-solving—it identifies a less-than-ideal condition and a proposed solution that ought to be done.

- ◆ Innovative—it is a nice-to-be-done activity that will result in something better, faster, cheaper, easier, or safer.

To classify your goals, create a list of goal statements for each goal type.

Essential goals	Essential goal A Essential goal B Essential goal C, etc.
Problem-solving goals	Problem-solving goal A Problem-solving goal B Problem-solving goal C, etc.
Innovative goals	Innovative goal A Innovative goal B Innovative goal C, etc.

This provides a workable list of identified goals to be achieved.

Goal statements may overlap into multiple types.

For example: "Learn the Spanish language with sufficient fluency to be able to carry on a complete conversation with a fluent friend and be able to translate my newsletter into Spanish for the Hispanic IBOs in my organization."

This innovative goal to learn Spanish takes on an additional problem-solving motive if knowing Spanish would enable you to better communicate with Hispanic IBOs in your organization. One motive is purely self-improvement, while accomplishing the goal also solves a business problem.

When this occurs, you need to classify overlapping statements by the highest level of need.

Goal Type	Level of Need
Essential	Must be done
Problem-solving	Ought to be done
Innovative	Nice to be done

For example: A combination essential and problem-solving goal should be classified as an *essential* goal because it must be done and therefore has the highest level of need.

Likewise, an essential/innovative goal is classified as an essential goal. A problem-solving/innovative goal would be included in the *problem-solving list* because "ought to be done" is a more critical need than "nice to be done."

The key to the correct classification of goal statements is to remember that some goals must be done, while others ought to be done and still others would be nice to be done.

 Define a goal any way you want: 'the end result,' 'the ultimate intent,' 'the objective of your labor,' 'the target at which you're aiming,' 'the result of achievement toward which your labor is directed.' Getting your goal clear in your mind is the first step in making a dream real, workable, possible. And for business, one primary goal is profit. "

—from **Compassionate Capitalism**
by Rich DeVos

ESTABLISH STANDARDS FOR PERFORMANCE

The next necessary step in goal development is to identify a standard for performance that indicates the level of results expected for each goal. Standards of performance serve two purposes:

♦ They indicate progress made toward the goal

♦ They tell when the goal has been achieved

It is important that these standards be established before any activities begin. They represent specific objectives or milestones to be reached during progress toward goals. Specific times must be established to indicate when progress will be measured–in future days, weeks, months, or years.

Three separate standards for performance should be established:

Minimal: Indicates that some progress has been made toward goal achievement, but may not be at a pace sufficient to guarantee goal achievement.

Acceptable: Progress made is consistent with goal achievement during the time allotted.

Outstanding: More progress than expected was achieved when measured at the milestone date.

For example, if the goal is:

"Increase my personal sponsoring from 1 per month to 15 per year, by March 31 (nine months from now)."

then standards for performance might be as follows:

Performance Standard		Performance Level
1 new IBO per month within 3 months	=	*Minimal*
2 new IBOs per month within 3 months	=	*Acceptable*
3 new IBOs per month within 3 months	=	*Outstanding*

Standards of performance that serve as objectives will indicate progress by specifying:

♦ When improvement is expected

♦ What the situation will be after it is improved

Proper standards for comparison include a time element for review ("within three months") and a quantifiable standard for progress ("3 new IBOs per month").

IDENTIFY OBSTACLES TO GOAL ACHIEVEMENT

There may be obstacles that block the way to goal achievement and must be overcome in order to reach the goal. Obstacles are a real barrier to goal achievement. It makes no difference if the barrier is tangible, or solely in one's own mind—the barrier is real. Therefore, it is very important to:

♦ Identify the obstacle to achievement of the goal

♦ Plan a way to overcome the obstacle

Some examples of obstacles which are barriers to goal achievement are:

Goal: "Increase my personal sponsoring by adding 15 new IBOs per year by March 31 this year."

Obstacle: You just moved to a new city within the last 6 months.

Obstacle: You are inexperienced in prospecting techniques.

Obstacle: You may have a big project coming up at work that will take more of your time each week.

It is important to anticipate the possibility of these obstacles and have a plan of action. When you take the necessary actions, you will avoid a major roadblock to goal achievement. Planning for these possibilities may mean the difference between abandoning and achieving your goal.

OVERCOMING OBSTACLES EXERCISE

What steps could be planned to overcome any of the above listed obstacles? Write your thoughts here.

_____

_____

_____

_____

_____

Avoid Unproductive Activities

The most dangerous obstacle to goal achievement is unproductive activities. This obstacle is a form of procrastination, but it is more dangerous because it is harder to detect than procrastination.

Unproductive activities appear to be relevant to goal accomplishment, but in fact they do not actually help achieve the goal. Such activities might include:

- Researching and reviewing all possible sponsoring techniques beyond the point of satisfaction, before beginning to execute action plans

- Spending time on the phone without a plan for what you want to accomplish

- Talking to prospects daily without offering them the opportunity to see the plan

Each of these may be very good and necessary activities and may need to be part of the overall plan for goal achievement. However, they do not directly contribute to goal achievement.

The only activities that are relevant are those included as objectives in the goal-achievement planning process. Simply doing something every day gives the appearance of performing activity toward reaching the goal. However, unless the individual is truly focused on the goal itself (not just on any activity), the time and resources invested may be wasted. The effort may not be directed toward the specific, established goal.

Methods for avoiding unproductive activities include:

- Establishing clear, focused goal statements

- Performing only those activities that meet objectives and that result in goal achievement

- Continually reviewing the results, priorities, and plans that lead to established goals

DETERMINE W.I.I.F.M. (WHAT'S IN IT FOR ME?)

One critical element for success is determining, "What's in it for me–how do I directly benefit from achieving this goal?" People who are committed to achieving goals that they helped create are even more committed to goals that benefit them personally, even in a business environment.

Monetary incentives, recognition, pride, and self-improvement are all good motivators. People perform better when they are convinced that there are personal benefits that can result from accomplishing a goal.

When you develop business goals, it's important to identify any personal advantages or benefits as well. For personal goals, you must first convince yourself of the benefits if you expect to adequately perform the tasks necessary for goal achievement. For example:

Goal	W.I.I.F.M.
"Lose those last ten pounds."	"I'll get to wear all those clothes that don't fit now."
"Learn a new PC software program."	"I can do my job faster and it will give me more time with my group."

Commitment to goal achievement sometimes means looking at the goal from a more selfish perspective.

" To achieve goals demands hard work, determination, and commitment. For many, though, the main reason they do not establish a quest to achieve goals is plain fear; the fear of ridicule from others or the fear of defeat. Others fear their goals will not be perfect—or worse still, they may consider themselves presumptuous. "

—from **Soaring with Eagles**
by Bill Newman

RECAP OF TASK 3

There are five important steps in goal development:

1. **Classify goals by type:**

   ♦ Essential: Must be done

   ♦ Problem-solving: Ought to be done

   ♦ Innovative: Nice to be done

2. **Prioritize your goals:**

   ♦ Essential goals are more important than...

   ♦ Problem-solving goals, which are more important than...

   ♦ Innovative goals

   Rank goals within each category based on relative importance, time sequence, and cost/benefit relationship.

3. **Establish standards of performance that include:**

   ♦ An established time for review of progress

   ♦ A quantitative method for determining progress:
   Minimal: Some progress
   Acceptable: Enough progress
   Outstanding: More than expected progress

4. **Identify all obstacles to goal achievement:**

   Formulate contingency plans for overcoming potential obstacles.

5. **Determine W.I.I.F.M. (What's In It For Me?)**

   There must always be a personal motive identified to ensure motivation toward goal achievement, especially in the business environment.

" Success is the progressive realization of predetermined, worthwhile goals, stabilized with balance and purified by belief. "

—from **Chart Your Way to Success**
by Glenn Bland

EXAMPLES OF TASK 3

Remember: Goal development expands the goal statement to provide context and substance for the expected results and benefits. Let's demonstrate the five steps in goal development.

Goal Statement: "Learn the Spanish language with sufficient fluency to be able to carry on a complete conversation with a fluent friend or a Spanish-speaking IBO by June 30, two years from now, within a cost for books, materials, and courses not to exceed $1,500."

Classification:

Problems Solving/Innovative, Nice-to-Do but also solves a problem. "There is no pressure to learn Spanish. I want to learn the language in order to make it easier to travel in Mexico and visit Mexico City. However learning it makes communicating with Spanish-speaking IBOs easier, making this ordinarily nice-to-do goal something that ought to be done."

Priority:

"I cannot quit my job to study Spanish full time; therefore, my first priority is my job. However, in terms of my free time, I would like to give this a very high priority. I am willing to devote one night per week to formal Spanish classes."

Standards of Performance:

♦ "If I learn Spanish at least one night per week, after six months, I should be able to listen to and understand at least 50 percent of a conversation with a Spanish-speaking IBO"

♦ "After one year, I should understand 75 percent of what is said and participate somewhat in the conversation"

♦ "After 18 months, I should be able to understand a conversation totally and fully participate in discussion"

♦ "After two years, I will converse fluently with Spanish-speaking IBOs with little difficulty"

Obstacles:

Example: Finding an effective training or school.

How to overcome: Seek out references and conduct an investigation and interviews for possible schools.

Example: Work responsibilities may conflict with course schedule.

How to overcome: Discuss with teacher and get assignments ahead of travel; arrange make-up classes; postpone unnecessary travel.

Example: "Learning a foreign language is difficult. I never studied language in high school or college."

How to overcome: Sit in on a class to determine how difficult it will be to study; recognize that people do learn languages. Commit yourself to studying and doing what is necessary to learn the language.

What's in it for me?:

"After achieving this goal, I will be bilingual. I will be able to travel to Mexico and Spain with more confidence; even more importantly, I will have a skill that helps me in my business through better communication with Spanish-speaking IBOs."

Task 4: Formulate Action Plans

The final task of the goal-setting process incorporates Tasks 1 and 3 into a workable action plan. This plan details the activities and actions necessary to accomplish the goal. Action plans organize thoughts into logical and executable action items (objectives). They describe the objectives to be reached and the tactics to be used to achieve the desired expectations for each goal. When objectives and tactics are incorporated into a workable action plan, goal achievement is more likely to occur.

The formulation of a goal-oriented action plan starts with identifying opportunities for goal achievement (Task 1), creating S.M.A.R.T. goal statements that are correctly constructed and documented (Task 2) and fully developing goals (Task 3).

The first step in the creation of a written action plan is final review of the goal information available to ensure that it is complete, clear, and realistic enough to serve as the foundation for focused action and activity. When you have gathered the basic material for each goal and goal statement, ask the following questions:

- ◆ Is the goal complementary to the mission? Does it contribute to the overall purpose?

- ◆ Is the goal realistic? Is it practical, achievable, and possible?

- ◆ Did the individuals responsible for achieving the goal participate in its creation? (Commitment is a component of success.)

- ◆ Have outcomes been quantified so that progress can be measured? This should include when and how much progress is expected.

- ◆ Are the objectives defined for reaching the goal? How will the goal be achieved?

- ◆ Are sufficient resources committed for reaching the goal? Resources should include the required people, finances, time, commitment, etc.

- ◆ Are potential obstacles to the goal identified? Have contingency plans been designed?

If you can answer "yes" to each of these questions, then the action plan will provide a road map to goal achievement.

Each of the above elements will be scattered throughout the working papers and goal statements developed in the earlier tasks of the goal-setting process.

The purpose of formulating an action plan is to provide order and organization to the important details of each goal. Order and organization are best achieved using the action-planning form shown on the next page. This form helps to create a road map to goal accomplishment.

GOAL ACTION FORM

Once a review is finished and there is reasonable assurance that all (or most) of the necessary goal-oriented details exist, then the Goal Action Form can be completed. It is useful because it documents the action plan for goal achievement.

GOAL ACTION FORM

Goal:	Rationale for this goal:

Action Plan: (steps/procedures, assignments)   **Deadlines:**

1. _____   1. _____

_____

2. _____   2. _____

_____

3. _____   3. _____

_____

4. _____   4. _____

_____

Projected results: (success indicators)

❑ Immediate: _____

❑ Long term: _____

Obstacles/constraints:

Cost: (resources/time)

Person responsible:	Completion date

COMPLETING THE GOAL ACTION FORM

There are eight separate entry areas of the Goal Action Form. Each information element was outlined, defined, or acquired during the earlier tasks of opportunity identification, goal statement creation, and goal development. The information required is:

1. Goal

Enter the actual goal statement created in Task 2. This statement contains S.M.A.R.T. goal elements: specific, measurable, action-oriented, realistic, and time- and resource-constrained.

2. Rationale for this goal

This is the goal benefit outlined in Task 1, Opportunity Identification; it describes the importance of the goal to the mission as a guide to the rationale.

If the goal type is:

- ♦ Essential: The goal is necessary for continued growth and progress of the business or individual

- ♦ Problem-solving: Proposes a more appropriate or desired condition than the condition that exists. It eliminates a problem that hinders growth, progress, creativity, improvement, etc.

- ♦ Innovative: Makes something already good or satisfactory quantifiably better, faster, cheaper, easier, safer, etc.

The goal rationale should also include the W.I.I.F.M. (What's In It For Me?) identified in goal development. The personal benefit to goal achievement (especially in a business environment) is an important motivator that ensures success.

3. **Action plan (steps/procedures/assignments)**

This lists the specific objectives that must be met. This is the most important aspect of the action plan because it outlines the specific and measurable steps to take to reach the goal, as well as the methods to be used. This section should also include the approaches (tactics) necessary to satisfy the needs for goal achievement.

Deadlines—provide a time limitation allowed for completion of objectives and the goal. Precise deadlines encourage activity and establish the priority of each objective.

4. **Projected results (success indicators)**

These are the long- and short-term expected results that indicate progress and/or completion of the action plans and the goal. These quantifiable elements provide a standard for comparison and milestones for measuring progress.

5. **Obstacles/constraints**

These are the potential obstacles that could block progress to the goal. Include the contingency plan and tactics necessary to overcome these obstacles.

6. **Cost (resources/time)**

State the allowable expense for achieving the goal in time and resources to be used. A time and resource constraint ensure that an acceptable return on investment exists for this goal.

7. **Person responsible**

This identifies who is responsible for achieving the goal. You can participate in achieving specific objectives, but only you can be held accountable for goal accomplishment.

8. **Completion date**

State the exact date and time for goal completion. This information is part of a properly constructed goal statement.

The completed Goal Action Form organizes the various elements of the goal into an orderly, workable road map for goal achievement. It provides a visual representation (and reminder) of all the actions, activities, expected results, timing, benefits, responsibilities, and contingencies of a well-planned goal.

RECAP OF TASK 4

Action plans bring all the elements of goals together to create a useful road map to goal achievement.

Achievement of goals has a better chance for success when the goals are:

- ♦ Clear, realistic, and complementary to the mission
- ♦ Correctly constructed and documented
- ♦ Properly developed
- ♦ Supported by workable objectives
- ♦ Incorporated into a written action plan

Goal Action Forms are helpful devices for organizing the diverse elements of goals into a complete and integrated package.

The form provided on page 63 provides a handy reference and reminder sheet for ensuring goal accomplishment.

 You should have a series of goals that will meet your needs and desires for each particular phase of your life. Events, circumstances, and situations change. And if your goals can't change as well, then you are bound to become frustrated and discouraged. Why? Because you haven't adjusted your goals to reflect the changes in your life. As a result, you no longer have direction.

—from **Born to Win**
by Lewis Timberlake

Remember: The action plan is your road map to goal achievement. Plan each step. Clearly define and state the actions and activities for reaching your goal. A plan helps you take action in a way that ensures goal achievement.

MARY & JACK

Does goal setting work? Mary and Jack have no doubt that setting goals has made all the difference in their Amway business. Although they filled their lives with activities their upline said made up the system, in the early years they just didn't seem to be headed in the direction they wanted to go. When they stopped wishing they could build their Amway business and put their plans in writing—in specific details, not generalities, things started to happen.

They set their sights on the desired end result. They figured out exactly how many business plans they needed to show, how many products they needed to sell, and how many IBOs they needed to help build their own businesses. How did they keep track of what they had to do and what kind of progress they were making? They wrote down their goals and checked them on a regular basis to make sure that what they were doing was moving them closer to the end result.

P A R T

3

GOAL
ACHIEVEMENT

The Foundation and Support for Goal Achievement

The four tasks—(1) identify opportunities, (2) write goal statements, (3) develop goals, and (4) formulate action plans—are only the foundation and support activities for goal achievement. They lay the groundwork for goal achievement by setting the stage for success.

Goals are achieved only through actions and activities. Plans and planning are very important parts of the goal-achievement process. Good planning can tell you how and where to go—but it won't help you succeed unless you put the plan into action.

There are three action elements necessary to ensure goal achievement:

1. **Implement the plan—the strategies, procedures, activities, etc.**

2. **Monitor progress made at specific intervals.**

3. **Revise action plans as necessary.**

When executed properly, these three elements create a self-correcting loop for goal accomplishment.

Implement the Plan

Planning is a good start on the road to goal accomplishment. The new ideas, procedures, strategizies, and activities, however, must be implemented for progress to be made. Without action, nothing is achieved.

It is easier to take action when you have completed the Goal Action Form, because it serves as the road map that specifies who, what, when, how, and how much for each goal.

Who is assigned the responsibility for coordinating and executing the activities needed for reaching your *objectives*.

What is to be accomplished.

When the activity must be completed.

How the goal will be achieved and what obstacles/constraints could block achievement of the goal.

How much is the cost in dollars, resources, and time to be invested in achieving the goal.

All the elements of the Goal Action Form outline the actions necessary for goal accomplishment. However, only real actions and activities will accomplish the goal.

The Chinese have a proverb,

The journey of a thousand miles starts with but a single step.

Goals cannot be achieved solely through planning and wishing. Goal accomplishment requires action and implementation of the positive strategies, procedures, and activities that make it possible to achieve the desired goal.

Monitor Progress

Achieving the established objectives and goals requires careful periodic monitoring of the actions taken and the measurable results of the actions.

Monitoring confirms that time and effort are productive in achieving the intended results. Also, when you monitor actions and progress, you will see which tactics work best.

The quantifiable and measurable standards of performance established in the goal statement and the milestones (dates) set for review help provide tangible ways to monitor progress.

It is important to set the monitoring milestones at practical and planned intervals. They should be clear and precise calendar dates for review that can be understood by those who are responsible for accomplishing action plans.

The Goal Action Form serves as an excellent checklist for monitoring progress toward objective and goal achievement. Each of these planned elements can be used periodically to review the actual progress made (plan vs. actual).

The monitoring function is a very important element in goal accomplishment because it will indicate whether midcourse adjustments to action plans and tactics are needed to ensure success.

Revise Objectives/Action Plans

To achieve your goals, you sometimes have to revise your objectives/action plans and tactics, because the actions and activities taken do not always produce results exactly as planned. Sometimes results fall short of planned expectations.

Part of goal development (Task 3) was to identify obstacles to goal achievement and methods for overcoming each potential obstacle. Even with proper planning and established contingency plans, new, unidentified obstacles occur that require changes in direction or method to reach the goal. It may be vitally important to the ultimate achievement of the goal to revise your objectives and tactics.

It's very important to note that the goals themselves should not be changed. The goal is important, or it would not be this far along in the process. The monitoring activity outlined above will identify the most effective tactics—those that produce the most beneficial results.

Circumstances change and so should the plans, objectives, and tactics you use to achieve worthwhile goals. Continually review and revise your Goal Action Form (ideally, once every three months for long-term goals). This creates a useful and dynamic work plan for accomplishing your goals.

Goal achievement occurs only when the following two major and seven minor elements are present:

I. Comprehensive Goal Foundation

1. Identified goal opportunities

2. S.M.A.R.T. goal statements

3. Complete goal development

4. Written action plan

II. Goal Achievement Activities

5. Implement program

6. Monitor results

7. Revise plan

The cycle of implementing, monitoring and revising should be executed over and over during the goal achievement process. When you revise your action plans and tactics, you then have to implement a new set of strategies, procedures, and activities. This implementation is followed by additional monitoring activities at scheduled intervals that result in additional revisions, followed by new implementations, monitoring… and so on until each goal is achieved.

This cycle must occur as often as necessary to draw closer to achieving your goals. The cycle ends only when the goal is reached.

MARY & JACK Mary and Jack are now able to enjoy the fruits of their efforts, and they focus on helping others develop their own Amway businesses. They have learned that the key that opens the doors to success is knowing what they want and making certain that they set deadlines for accomplishing their goals. They have learned through years of experience that a person's life can't go according to plan if the person has no plan.

Today, Mary and Jack have a very successful Amway business that keeps growing even while they travel to parts of the world far from their home. Even though they are successful beyond many people's dreams, they have learned that they must still set goals. And, their goals get bigger and better each year. They still write them down in S.M.A.R.T. terms. After all, Mary and Jack realize that "It's not enough to make progress; they must make it in the right direction."

Part III Summary

Goals are achieved only through action and activity. The three actionable elements that ensure goal achievement are:

Implement the plan

The who, what, when, how, and how much definitions of action and activities are necessary for goal achievement. This represents the physical execution of the activities.

Monitor progress

Review of progress toward goal achievement. Comparing your plan with actual progress. The use of quantifiable expected results and specific milestones dates for review.

Revise objectives/action plans

Revision of the action plans and tactics when change is indicated. Use tactics that work and draw you closer to your goal. Do not revise the goal; change only the means to achieving the goal—the objectives and tactics. Determine what works and what doesn't. Revise the action plan to be more productive.

> When you believe something is impossible, your mind goes to work for you to prove why. But, when you believe, really believe, something can be done, your mind goes to work for you and helps you find the ways to do it.
>
> —from **The Magic of Thinking Big**
> by David J. Schwartz

PART

4

SUMMARY

Book Summary

What is a goal?

A goal is a specific and measurable accomplishment to be achieved within a specified time and under specific time/resource constraints.

Goals are written statements of intent and results to be achieved. These statements contain:

♦ Action verbs

♦ Measurable outcomes

♦ Specific dates for accomplishment

♦ Time and resource constraints

Mission statements define your cause and provide direction for goals.

Objectives/action plans are tactics used to achieve goals. They must be complementary to the goal and the mission.

Why set goals?

Well-defined goals enable people to choose, design, and implement their life and work objectives to achieve a mission or life purpose.

Goals will:

♦ Establish direction

♦ Identify results

♦ Improve teamwork

♦ Heighten performance

Who sets goals?

The people involved in achieving the goal should help set the goal to ensure success. People are committed to achieving goals that they help create.

How are goals set?

Creating goals is a four-task process:

1. **Identify opportunities for goals that evolve from what**

   ♦ "MUST BE DONE"–Essential GOALS

   ♦ "OUGHT TO BE DONE"–Problem-Solving GOALS

   ♦ "NICE TO HAVE DONE"–Innovative GOALS

2. **Write S.M.A.R.T. goal statements**

   ♦ Specific: Detailed, particular, focused

   ♦ Measurable: Quantifiable, limiting

   ♦ Action-oriented: Produce results

   ♦ Realistic: Practical, achievable

   ♦ Time- and resource-constrained: Scheduled, regulated by time and deadlines

3. **Develop goals**

   ♦ Classify goals by type

   ♦ Prioritize within each type

   ♦ Establish standards for performance

   ♦ Identify obstacles to goal achievement

   ♦ Determine "W.I.I.F.M." (What's in it for me?)

4. **Formulate action plans**

   ♦ Use the Goal Action Form as a road map to goal achievement.

How are goals achieved?

Goal achievement requires you to:

1. **Implement the plan**

   ♦ Planning must be careful and comprehensive

   ♦ Execute the plan

2. **Monitor progress**

   ♦ Measure planned vs. actual results

   ♦ Determine which elements work and do not work

3. **Revise objectives/action plans**

   ♦ Change tactics, not goals

   ♦ Apply what works

4. **Restart the cycle**

   ♦ Implement the plan

   ♦ Monitor progress

   ♦ Revise objectives

Continue until your goal is achieved. SUCCESS!

Answers to Exercises

GOAL ELEMENTS EXERCISE (p. 12)

1. Action verb: **increase**
   Measurable outcome: **15%, ten new businesses**
   Specific date: **December 31 of this year**
   Constraint: **per month**

2. Action verb: **gain/increase**
   Measurable outcome: **10 new customers, personal sales to $1,000**
   Specific date: **December 31 of this year**
   Constraint: **by getting referrals from existing customers**

3. Action verb: **Sponsor/teach**
   Measurable outcome: **Three new IBOs, 10 IBOs in depth**
   Specific date: **June 30 of this year**
   Constraint: **Working in each group two days per week**

SPECIFIC GOALS EXERCISE (p. 42)

Statements A, D, and G are too general. They state only broad "intents for action."

Statements B, E, and H are a little more specific, but not specific enough to be used in goal statements.

Statements C, F, and I are more specific and focus intent on a desired outcome.

MEASURABLE GOALS EXERCISE (p. 43)

Measurable outcomes:

A. No. The term "better" cannot be quantified as written. "Better" is a relative term and no indication is given as to what "better service" will mean for each specific customer.

B. Yes. "Two work days" is a measurable outcome. It can be determined whether an answer was or was not given in 2 days after it was received.

C. No. "Significantly" is too ambiguous a term for goals. It is relative to an undefined standard.

D. Yes. "Fifty percent of current levels" is measurable, assuming the number of complaints received is known.

E. No. "Only very" is not measurable or quantifiable.

REALISTIC GOALS EXERCISE (p. 46)

A. Realistic. Swimming a mile has been accomplished by many individuals. With practice, many people could achieve this goal.

B. Unrealistic. Swimming across the Pacific Ocean is unrealistic, even for expert swimmers.

C. Unrealistic. Holding your breath until you faint is possible and achievable, but it is impractical and therefore unrealistic. If there were a legitimate purpose for holding your breath until you faint, then perhaps this activity could be classified as realistic.

D. Realistic. Learning to play the piano is also an activity that has been demonstrated and is achievable.

THE STRETCH PRINCIPLE EXERCISE (p. 46)

The new IBO will work toward the goal of Direct by following the system established by those who have already accomplished that and higher levels. With persistence and increased dedication to showing the plan, listening to tapes, reading, attending seminars, and keeping the dream in sight, each new level can be achieved.

TIME-CONSTRAINED GOALS EXERCISE (p. 48)

Statements B, F and G are specific enough to represent deadlines.

Statements A and C are too general to be deadlines.

Statements D and E at first appear to be deadlines, but unfortunately the words "first thing" and "before the close" can be interpreted differently by different people.

Deadlines for goals must leave no room for interpretation.

Bibliography

Bland, Glenn. *Chart Your Way to Success*. Wheaton, Illinois: Tyndale House Publishers, Inc., 1972. (BK393)

Covey, Stephen R. *The 7 Habits of Highly Effective People: Powerful Lessons in Personal Change*. New York: Simon & Schuster, Inc., 1989. (BK372)

DeVos, Rich. *Compassionate Capitalism: People Helping People Help Themselves*. New York: Dutton, Division of Penguin Books USA Inc., 1993. (BK391)

Engstrom, Ted W. *The Pursuit of Excellence*. Grand Rapids: Zondervan Publishing House, 1981 (BK401)

Schwartz, David J. *The Magic of Thinking Big*. New York: Simon & Schuster, Inc., 1987. (BK66)

Timberlake, Lewis. *Born to Win*. Wheaton, Illinois: Tyndale House Publishers, Inc., 1986. (BK308)

Waitley, Denis. *The Winner's Edge*. New York: Times Books, 1980. (BK188)

Yager, Dexter and Ron Ball. *Everything I Know at the Top I Learned at the Bottom*. Wheaton, Illinois: Tyndale House Publishers, Inc., 1991. (BK351)

Yager, Dexter R. Sr., with Doyle Yager. *The Business Handbook: A Guide to Building Your Own Successful Amway Business*. Charlotte: InterNET Services Corporation, 1985. (BK247)

NOTES:

NOTES:

NOTES:

NOTES:

NOTES: